COLDPLAY LIVE

7777 W. BLUEMOUND RD. P.O. BOX 13819 MILWAUKEE, WI 53213

Visit Hal Leonard Online at
www.halleonard.com

Politik

Words & Music by Guy Berryman, Jon Buckland, Will Champion & Chris Martin

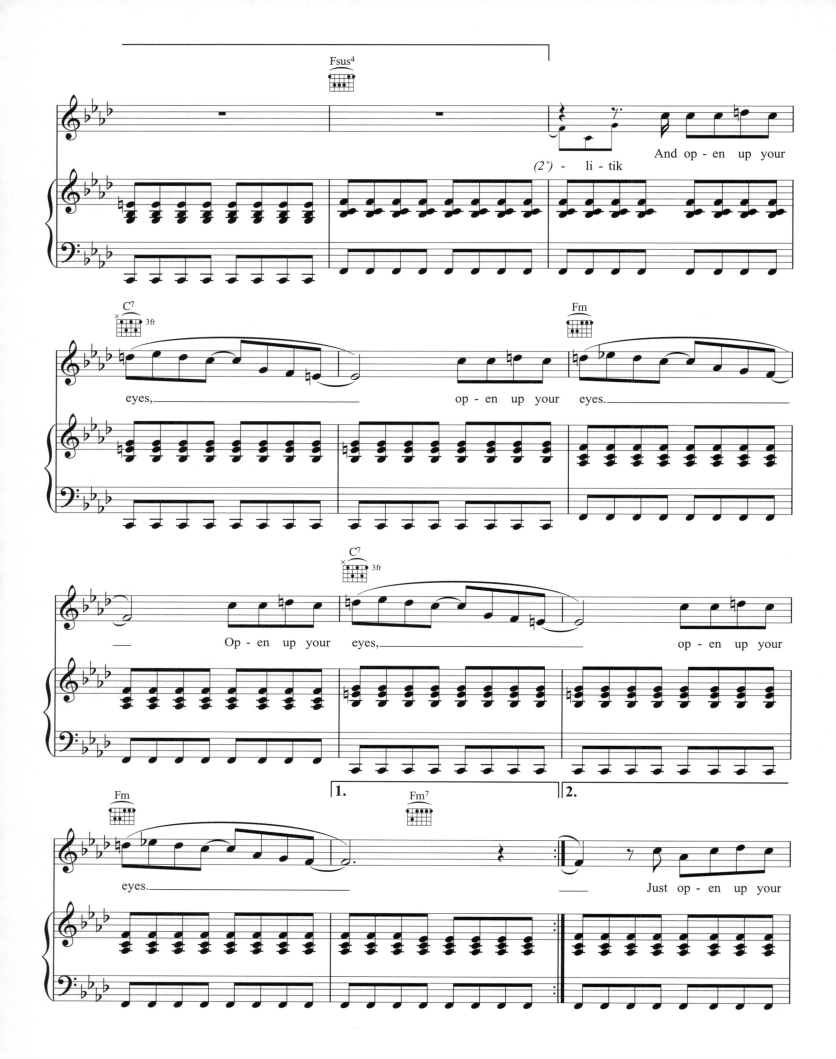

eyes.

Give me love ov- er

2° Instrumental

love ov- er love ov- er this,___ ahh___

11

Verse 2:
Give me one, 'cause one is best
In confusion confidence
Give me peace of mind and trust
Don't forget the rest of us.
Give me strength, reserve, control
Give me heart and give me soul
Wounds that heal, and cracks that fix
Tell me your own politik.

And open up your eyes *etc.*

God Put A Smile Upon Your Face

Words & Music by Guy Berryman, Jon Buckland, Will Champion & Chris Martin

your guess_____ is as good____ as_____

mine._____

Guitar

Verse 2:
Where do we go to draw the line?
I've got to say I wasted all your time honey, honey
Where do I go to fall from grace?
God put a smile upon your face, yeah.

Verse 3:
Where do we go, nobody knows
Don't ever say you're on your way down, when
God gave you style and gave you grace
And put a smile upon your face.

Now when you work it out *etc.*

A Rush Of Blood To The Head

Words & Music by Guy Berryman, Jon Buckland, Will Champion & Chris Martin

do back the things it did to you in re-

-turn. Ha,

ha. Ha, ha.

3. He said I'm gon-na buy a gun and start a war

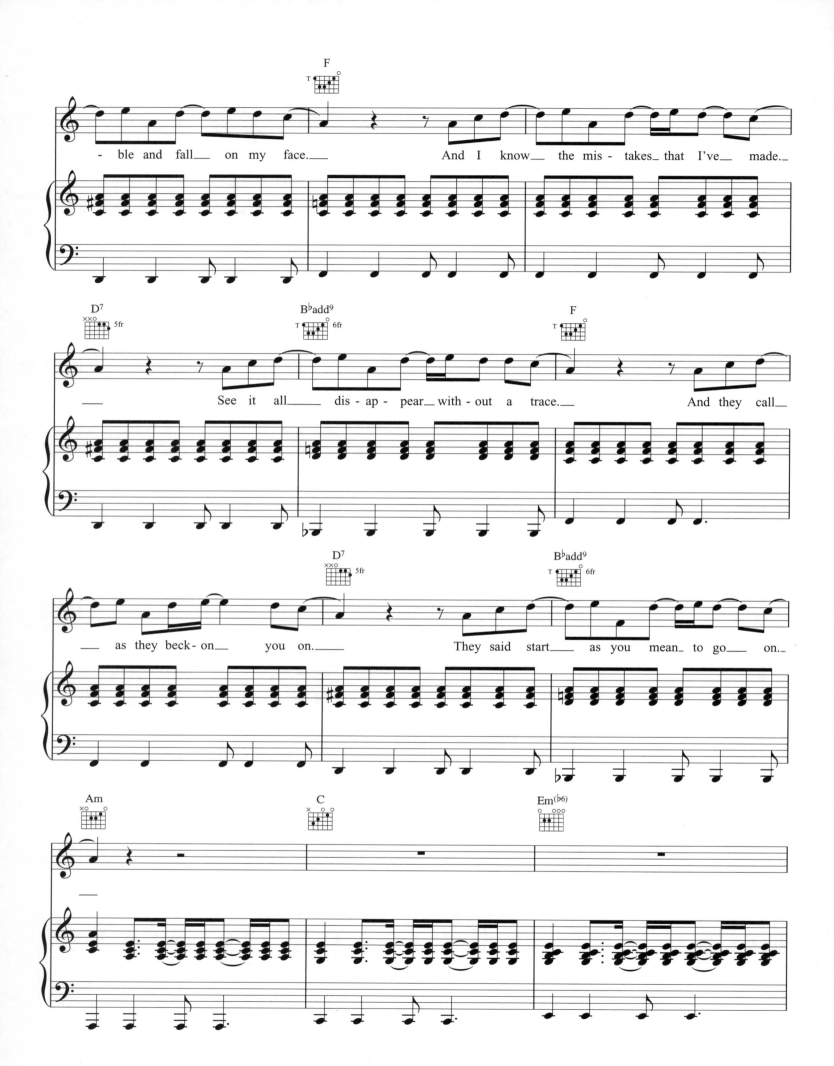

Oh, meet me on____ the road, oh, meet me where____ I____
____ said. Blame it all____ up-on_____ a rush of blood____ to the
head.

Daylight

Words & Music by Guy Berryman, Jon Buckland, Will Champion & Chris Martin

Verse 2:
On a hilltop
On a sky-rise
Like a first-born child
On the full tilt
And in full flight
Defeat darkness
Breaking daylight.

Ooh and the sun will shine *etc.*

Trouble

Words & Music by Guy Berryman, Jon Buckland, Will Champion & Chris Martin

and thought of all__ the stu - pid things I'd_ said.

2. Oh no, what's this? A spi - der web__ and I'm caught in the mid - dle.
3. Oh no, I see, a spi - der web__ and it's me in the mid - dle.

So I turned to run,_____ and thought of all__ the stu - pid things_ I'd_
So I twist, and_ turn,___ but here__ am I___ in my_ lit - tle__ bub -

They spun a web___

One I Love

Words & Music by Guy Berryman, Jon Buckland, Will Champion & Chris Martin

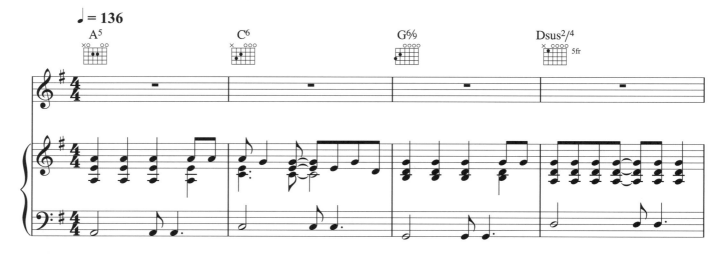

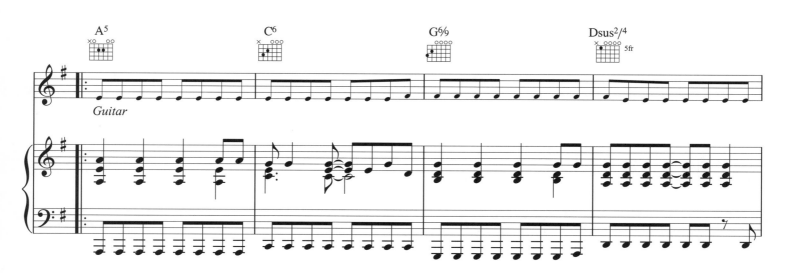

41

44

Sing oh,_____ oh,_____ oh._____

Sing - ing oh,_____ oh,_____ oh._____

Sing it to me oh,_____ oh,_____ oh._____

Sing it to me oh,_____ oh,_____ ah._____

Don't Panic

Words & Music by Guy Berryman, Jon Buckland, Will Champion & Chris Martin

1, 2. Bones, sink - ing like stones, all___ that we've fought___ for.___
(Verse 3 Instrumental)

Homes, pla - ces we've grown, all___ of us are

Oh, all— that I know, there's no-thing here to run from,— cos

yeah, ev - 'ry-bo- dy here's got some-bo-dy to lean on.—

49

Shiver

Words & Music by Guy Berryman, Jon Buckland, Will Champion & Chris Martin

Guitar tuned:

① = D♯   ④ = B
② = B   ⑤ = A
③ = G   ⑥ = E

1. So I

look in your di - rec - tion but you pay me no at - ten - tion— do you?—
(Verse 2 see block lyric)

And I

know you don't lis - ten to me cos you say you see straight through me— don't

you?

But on and on————

Verse 2:
So you know how much I need you
But you never even see me do you?
And is this my final chance of getting you?

But on and on, from the moment I wake *etc.*

See You Soon

Words & Music by Guy Berryman, Jon Buckland, Will Champion & Chris Martin

1. So you lost your trust, and you nev-er should have,
2. So they came for you, they come snap-ping at your

I'll be do-in' my__ best,__ and I'll__ see you soon.__

And in a te-le-scope__ lens_____ and when all__ you want's__ friends__

I'll see you soon.__

1.

Moses

Words & Music by Guy Berryman, Jon Buckland, Will Champion & Chris Martin

Yellow

Words & Music by Guy Berryman, Jon Buckland, Will Champion & Chris Martin

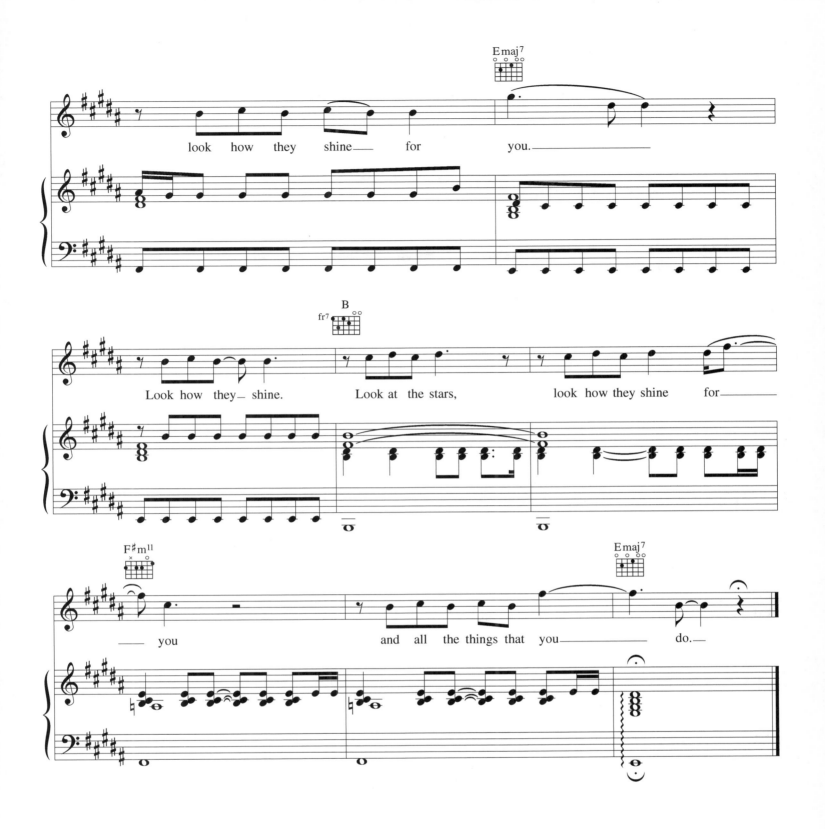

Verse 2:
I swam across, I jumped across for you
Oh, what a thing to do
Cos you were all yellow
I drew a line, I drew a line for you
Oh, what a thing to do
And it was all yellow.

Your skin, oh yeah, your skin and bones
Turn into something beautiful
And you know, for you I'd bleed myself dry
For you I'd bleed myself dry.

Everything's Not Lost

Words & Music by Guy Berryman, Jon Buckland, Will Champion & Chris Martin

hop - ing ev - 'ry -thing's   not   lost.

2.When you thought that it was___ ov-er,___ you could feel it all___ a-round. When ev'-ry-bo-dy's out___ to get you,___ don't you let it drag___ you down.___ So if you ev-er feel___ ne-glec - ted and if you think that all is lost,___

79

well, I'll be coun-ting up my____ de - mons yeah,_____

____ hop-ing ev - 'ry - thing's____ not lost.____

The Scientist

Words & Music by Guy Berryman, Jon Buckland, Will Champion & Chris Martin

1. Come up to meet__ you, tell you I'm sor - ry, you don't know how love-
(Verse 2 see block lyric)

Verse 2:
I was just guessing at numbers and figures
Pulling your puzzles apart.
Questions of science, science and progress
That must speak as loud as my heart.
Tell me you love me, come back and haunt me
Oh, and I rush to the start
Running in circles, chasing our tails
Coming back as we are.

Nobody said it was easy *etc.*

Clocks

Words & Music by Guy Berryman, Jon Buckland, Will Champion & Chris Martin

1. The lights go out and I can't be saved, tides that I tried to
(Verse 2 see block lyric)

93

And no - thing else com - pares.

And no - thing else com - pares.

Verse 2:
Confusion that never stops
The closing walls and the ticking clocks
Gonna come back and take you home
I could not stop that you now know, singing...
Come out upon my seas
Cursed missed opportunities
Am I a part of the cure?
Or I am a part of the disease, singing...

You are *etc.*

In My Place

Words & Music by Guy Berryman, Jon Buckland, Will Champion & Chris Martin

1. In my place, in my____ place were lines that I____ could-n't
(Verse 2 see block lyric)

Verse 2:
I was scared, I was scared
Tired and under-prepared
But I'll wait for it.
And if you go, if you go
And leave me down here on my own
Then I'll wait for you, yeah.

Yeah, how long must you wait *etc.*

Amsterdam

Words & Music by Guy Berryman, Jon Buckland, Will Champion & Chris Martin

my star is fad - ing and I _____ swerve out of con - trol._____

If____ I'd____ if I'd on - ly wait - ed I'd not be stuck here in this___

____ hole._____

2. Come here, oh,
(Verse 3 see block lyric)

Verse 3:
Come on, oh, my star is fading
And I see no chance of release
And I know I'm dead on the surface
But I am screaming underneath.

And time is on your side *etc.*

Life Is For Living

Words & Music by Guy Berryman, Jon Buckland, Will Champion & Chris Martin

I nev-er meant to do you wrong,_____ well that's what I came_ here to say._

And if I was wrong then I'm sor - ry,____ don't let it stand in our__ way. 'Cause my head just aches when I think of_____ the things that I should - n't have done.___ 'Cause life is for liv - ing, we all know____ and I don't want to live it a - lone._

I sing ah_____ and I sing ah._____

Yeah I sing ah._____

Guitar

'Cause in the end there's on - - - ly us.

AM980155-6/06(59046)